This book is dedicated to my wife Helen who was for a long time, in practice a single parent, never knowing when or indeed whether I would come home.

INTRODUCTION

With the ever changing face of policing some of the skills and tricks of the trade learnt through experience and passed down from generation to generation may be lost. Many are of course obsolete, others remain as valid today as they were 1839. This book explores a wide range of both old and new tools that the modern police officer have at their disposal.

No matter how long a police officer has been in the job they will find useful information within the various chapters of this book. The chapters are meant as an introduction to the subjects. Nobody could learn problem solving, public speaking, project management or restorative justice by reading a single chapter of a book. It's important that you build on the knowledge you gain from reading this book, and then enhance it by further reading, formal and informal training, and hands on experience.

Not all chapters will be relevant to everyone. For instance if you studied politics you would know the different types of politicians and what they do. If you don't think that a particular chapter will be of use to you, then skip it and go on to the next one. I'm convinced that you will regular dip into this book to support your work as you become a more effective and efficient police officer.

KEY LOCATIONS, KEY PEOPLE , KEY TIMES

The public frequently say they never see a police officer, that they want a visible presence, the reassurance of a uniformed police officer patrolling the streets where they live and work.   It is not, however, enough to just walk down a street to be a visible presence. Many senior officers believe it is enough to place officers in an inaptly named high visibility jacket for the public to notice them and gain instant reassurance, and to deter criminal activity. Whilst this may be true to a small extent, the fact that so many people walk into trees, lamp posts and other street furniture, or bump into other people is proof that there is more to being visible that just being present, even if it is in loud clothing.

The vast amount of people in a busy high street will not notice the patrolling officer. Their view will be blocked by other individuals and the natural environment. In addition to this there are so many other distractions and information to take in so people often will not register the presence of a patrolling officer. Similarly an officer patrolling a quiet residential street will not be seen by those at work, those busy doing housework or watching television. In other words patrolling without interaction does not make you a visible presence.

What the police officer needs to do is increase the chances of being seen, of being a visible presence by being seen and interacting with key people, in key locations, at key times.

Key people are the ones that make up your communities and in particular the community leaders. Key people communicate with others in their community and as a result they will have an influencing effect on them.

Key locations are those where people gather and have a few moments to spare, examples of these would be a commuter station in the morning, a primary school as parents drop their children off in the morning. Prize giving at schools, public events such as fetes, conferences, open days, and club meetings.

Key times are those when individuals have the time and space to interact and engage with the officer. It is also whenever the media is present. If an officer can get their visit at a location reported, preferably accompanied with their picture, in the press then their visibility increases as they are seen, by the residents they serve, in the living rooms, kitchens, and toilets of their homes. An individual may have never met you personally, but will know that you exist and patrol their area because you are always in the local paper, and their neighbours have mentioned having seen you.

But it is not just the law abiding that need to see you. A Police Officer will need to ensure that they are seen by the criminal element. Within criminal communities, not surprisingly there are key people, key locations, and key times.

Drug dealers and handlers of stolen property are examples of key people. They are in effect leaders within the criminal community. They will have a broad network of criminal contacts and if you are visible to them then the word will get out to the rest of the criminal community who, aware of your presence will find it harder to operate. You can obviously make it hard by active enforcement activity such as raids or use of stop and search powers, but you can also make it impossible for them to carry out their trade by just spending time with them. Handlers will not take in stolen property, drug dealers will not supply their wares whilst a police officer is talking to them. Of course there is the added bonus that a thief carrying stolen property may arrive and only notice you at the last moment; their actions will usually give ample suspicion for you to exercise your search powers.

The drug addict theif has a number of key locations; their home; their associates' homes; their car; other locations to do with their means of transport; their handlers and their drug dealers' places of operation. A thief will want to commit their crime in an area that is favourable to one or more of these locations. If you make the thief aware of your presence at these locations then you make it extremely difficult for them to operate.

The parking of a police car in a particular street can stop crime in that street whilst it is there. So if you are doing a routine non emergency call, park outside the handlers' or drug dealers' house and walk a short distance to the incident. Obvious really isn't it?

By knowing certain things about your local criminals you can organise your patrol so that they get to see you. Examples of this are benefit offices, or taking their kids to school.

Remember though you have to make sure they see you as an individual and that they feel threatened or uneasy by your presence. By this I don't mean that you should harass them, but rather you have to ensure that they know you are a honest, hardworking effective law enforcer, who happens to be everywhere they go. Performed correctly there is no reason that the criminal will not let their guard down and tell you things that they will later regret. Ultimately they want to keep you off their back.

You need to get the balance right between the time you spend raising your profile within the law abiding and the criminal communities, but you will need to spend time engaging with both. But be forewarned that the law abiding often find it hard to understand why you spend so much time passing long periods of time with criminals in a non-confrontational way.

COMMUNITY

What is community?

The dictionary definition of a community is both people living in the same area, or a group of people having cultural, religious or other characteristics in common. It's clear from this that in any particular neighbourhood there can be more than one community, and that individuals can be members of more than one of them at the same time.

Geographically individuals in the centre of a town will be a part of that town's community. As you look at people living further from a town centre you will find certain individuals who belong not to that particular town, their nearest, but to a neighbouring one. In other words there is an overlap. The more different the towns, the larger the overlap is likely to be. Then there are the non geographic communities, such as ethnic or religious groups, but they also include groups like businesses, clubs, arts, and other cultural reasons for individuals to group together to share a common interest or view. Some of these are of course now online or virtual communities.

It's worth pausing a while and thinking of the different communities that you belong to.

There will be individuals who do not fit into any community, they are isolated, sometimes not by choice. There will for example be individuals who belong to a non geographical community who feel isolated within the geographical area where they live because of a lack of contact with their non geographical community. These individuals will be hard to reach.

You may have heard of the expression "hard to reach communities," There is no such thing. Some communities are hard to engage with, operating in a firmly closed circle with rules or ethics that make it difficult for outsiders to communicate with them, but they are there and they are reachable.

Communities are flexible, constantly changing in size and shape. Communities adapt to circumstances and a police officer will need to be aware of issues that might prove to be the impetus for change. An issue that has been important to a community might almost overnight become insignificant, and likewise an issue that a community had no interest in might suddenly become very important.

A proposal to build a large airport will cause the local community to find a real and sudden interest in local wildlife. Individuals values will change. They will do and save whatever is necessary to survive.

As a police officer you need to identify the different communities in the area that you patrol. You need to understand them, understand their values, their needs, their desires, their issues. It is often desirable that you are accepted as an integral part of each community where this is not possible a community should at least view you as some significant use or value to them.

COMMUNITY LEADERS

Having identified the communities in your area, you'll need to identify who the leaders in each of them are. Some are easy to spot, local politicians for instance, the vicar or other religious head, the chair of the town partnership. Others are more difficult to spot, some don't even realise they are in fact community leaders.

Every street has somebody who, when push turns to shove, will stand up to be counted, meet the challenge, organise the protest, arrange a collection or petition when something good or bad happens. Everyone has the potential to be a leader they just need the right issue to stir them in to action.

Research on the internet, at the local library, with the local council, in the local media, in shop windows will identify many community leaders. Some, however, you will identify only when you stumble upon them unintentionally and only then if you are alert to the possibility of such an occurrence.

Are they truly representing the people they claim?

You will need to be aware of self appointed leaders who claim to represent everyone in their street, or to be the voice of a particular age group, or ethnic group. Although many have a genuine desire to act on behalf of those they claim to represent, some will instead be full of self importance and because of that they are not community leaders at all. They are merely vocal and represent their own views. Some start off with best intentions but change over time. This is not to say they are not worth listening to, or that what they are saying is wrong. You should however ensure that you take steps to ascertain how representative their views are by listening to others.   Even where the community has an elected leader you need to make sure that the view they are expressing is one that the community has given them the right to express on their behalf.

The better your understanding of how a community works, the more likely you are to be able to make use of them should the need arise, and the more likely they are to see you as someone who they can trust.

You will want to know how different communities in your area interact with each other. Faith communities are pretty active at building bridges with other faith communities. Local football and other sporting teams may all play in the same league and their managers meet regularly at meetings. Youth groups may come together for a particular event. Identifying the links and the potential links is important in comprehending how they work and cultivating trust.

Communities react differently as circumstances change. If an incinerator was to be built at a particular location the various leaders in each street would meet up and form a campaign committee, possibly joined by local councillors or "defenders" of the environment.

Your task as a police officer is to facilitate the linking of communities who would achieve more for the mutual benefit of all by working together on projects. Communities that work together gain a better understanding of each other reducing the likelihood of friction between them.

Consider two local secondary schools. If they have no regular contact and there is an isolated incident, such as a fight between a few pupils from each school this could quickly escalate to become a major problem. Rumours spread as pupils line up firmly behind those that attend their school. It can, as it has in the past, lead to large gangs forming and descending on the "rival" school with violent intent.

The same isolated incident between schools where there is regular contact and cooperation will not be blown out of proportion. Rumours are more likely to be squashed at an early stage by the facts. The allegiance to individual schools would be tempered by loyalty to individual pupils at the different schools.

POLITICIANS

A police officer needs to have an understanding of how the political process works. By knowing who does what you will be in a better position to interact with them in a productive manner. You need to know the responsibilities of the different types of politicians.

UK Parliament

The UK Parliament represents the people of the United Kingdom and has the power to make decisions and pass laws on a wide range of issues that affect you. It also debates major issues of the day; scrutinises government policy; protects the public and safeguards the rights of individuals; hears legal cases in the House of Lords

The UK Parliament is made up of the House of Commons and the House of Lords. The house of commons has 650 Members of Parliament (MPs.) Each MP represents a geographical area known as a constituency or seat. The political party with the most MPs usually forms the Goverment.   The Goverment proposes new laws and raises issues for Parliament to debate.   It also puts into action the decisions made by Parliament.

The House of Lords has around 700 members who scrutinise the work of the House of Commons.

The Queen although mostly ceremonial, has the role of approving the laws made by Parliament, and delivers the

Queens Speech that sets out what the Government plans to do each year.

Local Authorities

Local Authorities are responsible for providing local services and facilities. Councillors are elected to represent people who live in their wards at a local level. They set the strategy for the local authority.

The exact responsibilities of local authorities differs from area to area. But their responsibilities might include; housing; Education; Electoral registration; environmental health; Leisure and recreational facilities; libraries; local planning; local transport; parks and public spaces; regulation of local businesses; roads and footpaths; social services; waste and recycling; community safety; improving the health of the local population including delivery of drug and alcohol services and sexual health services.

It is important for you as a police officer to fully understand the responsibilities of your local authority.

What are councillors?

Each councillor is elected to represent an area known as a ward. Their role is to represent the interests of the local community and of the individuals that make up that community. Councillors are accountable to the public for the provision of services, for establishing the Council policies and for decisions taken at Council and committee meetings. Councillors are consulted by their constituents on a wide range of issues, where appropriate they will take the matter up on their behalf.

How Councils make decisions

Local Authorities must in law use one of these models:

- ◆ a mayor and cabinet executive

- ◆ a leader and cabinet executive

- ◆ the committee system

- ◆ other arrangements approved by the Secretary of State.

Whatever these arrangements are in your Local Authority
Councillors provide the democratic leadership of the council by representing members of the public, providing leadership and direction to the Local Authority, and scrutinising service delivery.

Council officers

Officers are employees of the council who

- ◆ implement the policies agreed by councillors ,

- ◆ organise and deliver services and

- ◆ provide unbiased, professional advice and support to councillors.

You will need to know who's who in your local authority. The roles and responsibilities of officers change frequently especially after elections if the Local Authority takes a new political direction.

Both Councillors and officers are only human and this means that some will be very set in their ways, whilst others will be open to new ideas.

The more you know what motivates an individual, the more you understand why they are in that particular role, what their limitations are both in law, and in personality.

PATROLLING

What is Patrolling?

Patrolling is the control of criminal activity and anti-social behaviour in a specific geographic area by movement through it, and it includes the interaction with both the law abiding and the criminal element.

You should take pride in your beat. You should have a number of aims;

- To ensure that no crime happens on your beat whilst you are on duty;

- To prevent serious crime from happening when you are not on duty;

- To be a reassuring presence allowing the local population to conclude that they live and work in an area that is safe and where everything is under control;

- To gather intelligence

To patrol effectively you should have as complete picture as possible of the area you are to patrol, including the things that might effect it.   You will need to keep that picture regularly updated. You will have the benefit of much information through technology available to you as you go about your work. You should aspire to gain a good healthy knowledge of the geography of your patch. A fuller picture can be obtained from a range of sources including intelligence reports, calls and letters from the public, local and national press, indeed from anyone who knows anything about the area or from anywhere else where relevant information may be found.

At the start of a tour you may have a number of tasks to perform. You may pick up further tasks during the course of the day. All these tasks need to be performed by you whilst at the same time you are preventing crime from happening.

Leading by example

As a uniform presence on the street a police officer is an important leader. Your actions may come under scrutiny. Follow simple rules like crossing a road at an appropriate place and in an appropriate way, such as a zebra crossing. Parking your vehicle legally will enhance the opinion people have of the police. Obeying the rules society lays down is important for a leader, it is what the public expects of the police, but you can go much further.

A really good leader will do more than is expected of them. When you walk down a street and see a bottle on a wall, don't just walk past it. Pick it up and place it in a bin. If you see an open gate to a children's playground you close it, a hole in the ground you place cones around it. When you see danger you'll need to remove it or at the very least reduce it. When you see a person needing a helping hand provide it. If you see something that might make people feel unsafe or uncomfortable you should do something to reduce the effect it is causing. You must lead by example and everything is in your remit providing it is lawful and makes the neighbourhood a better place to live and work in.

Patrolling should be unpredictable, yet have a purpose steered by local knowledge and intelligence. When you patrol from A to B you will be tempted to go the quickest or shortest route, but you should be extremely careful of always going the "usual" route.

There will be times when the shortest route is the most appropriate, for example you might be running late for a meeting or other appointment, however whenever possible the route from one place to another should be unpredictable, spontaneous, responding to circumstances, purposeful, and directed. You should vary your patrol to cover both below and above ground level where the environment allows this. You should be inventive, including dead ends, and stops. Your patrol should be both visible and invisible.

Let me expand. Your police station is next door to the town hall. You have to attend a meeting at the council office. The shortest route is to walk out of the front door of the police station walk a few yards down the road and into the front entrance of the town hall. The path between the two buildings is undoubtedly well trod. The crime level for this path would likely be non-existent. A better route would be to walk out of the police station, turn away from the town hall and perform an unpredictable patrol arriving in time for your meeting. Such a patrol will often add something to that meeting. It might provide the opportunity to speak to a few people and come to the meeting with an additional, different, surprising point of view, or with a quote that sums the situation up perfectly. If you know a particular location is going to come up during the meeting why wouldn't you go there immediately before hand so that you have a current impression of the place and the issue.

Of course the journey back to the police station should not be by the "usual route" either.

Criminals do not look up

It is a fact that criminals will always have a little look around before they commit a crime, they'll look to the front, the back and to the sides but they rarely look up. The same is of course true of most people, unless there is a particular reason such as a sudden noise why would you even glance upwards. When you are on patrol you should use this to your advantage. Find out what you can see from accessible roofs, from the communal windows tower blocks.. You never know when you might see something or be informed of some suspicious activity. It is far better that you know where you can get a view with the advantage of height before it is required.

Criminals also cannot see what ordinary people cannot see. As you walk along a street make note of how deep into each shop you can see. Where there is wooden fencing take time to look through any holes and gaps from both sides. Trees and street furniture also provide a degree of cover from being seen. As you patrol take in what you can and cannot see, and notice when someone gets hidden behind something.

Use the advantages of dark and light. It's obvious that a person in a shadow is harder to be seen than one who is lit up. So when you want to be seen walk in the light, when you want to be invisible walk in the dark.

Torches are useful to a police officer, but only if you use them properly. If you walk in to a dark alley with your torch on you will let people know you are there, giving them time to make good their escape. Instead of turning on your torch close your eyes for a second or two before entering the alley, walk a couple of paces into the alley before opening them again. Your eyes will instinctively adjust so that you are able to see without the need for any artifical light. Only use your torch once you have detained a suspect or to look for discarded property. Remember it is pointless you using this technique if you are working with a colleague who has their torch on, so teach them this before it becomes necessary to use it.

Criminals look but do not see

Have you ever wondered why in football a player will take a look around before skillfully passing the ball to an opposing player? They do this because they look but do not see. Criminals are no different they will often look around to see whether there is anybody who might interfere in the crime they are planning to commit, but because they don't really know what they are looking for they do not see anything that causes concern. If you use the natural cover you will be able to observe what they are doing, without them knowing. It is important to remember to always assume that you haven't been seen

Marking your beat

Whilst on patrol you should look for things that appear out of place or unusual. If you see an open door, an unlocked car, a broken window, unusual lights, or hear unusual noises you will rightly want to know more. However you also want to avoid doing what you don't have to do.   Marking your beat will help you achieve this, and reduce the amount of things you have to remember.

You will need to know if anything has changed since you last passed a particular area. A piece of black cotton tied at shin level across a dead end alley will be broken by anyone entering it. Providing it isn't broken you'll only need to go down there once before you set your mark.

A small stone balanced in the gap between the unhinged side of a gate and the gate post will fall to the floor when the gate is open. Likewise a piece of paper wedged between the door and its frame will drop when a door is opened. a stone on the wheel of a car will tell you if it has moved and returned, as would noting the position of the valve on a wheel. Marking a door or a gate can be useful to know when somebody is leaving an address.

Coordinated Patrolling

Whereas Single Patrolling is the default, there are opportunities available to enhance policing activity by co-ordinating those patrols with other officers. Officers patrolling together must be able to show that it adds value to an officer patrolling alone. Co-ordinated patrols can work in a number of ways;

Pulsing

Two officers patrol from one location to another but on route meet up or cross paths a number of times.

Attack

Attack a particular suspect or location by cutting off escape routes prior to engagement,

Trap

Follow suspects and guide them to where a colleague is waiting to interact.

Reinforcement

The police presence is reinforced by officers walking the same stretch of road shortly after one another. This can be done as often as necessary to reinforce the police presence

Observing

One officer can take up a position in cover and observe a developing situation then call on other officers to detain, arrest, or otherwise interact with people.

Link up
Link up with another officer to be more effective in dealing with suspects or witnesses.

Examples of Pulsing patrolling

Officers walking across an open space coming together at known problem areas like a wooded area or a playground.

Opposite sides of a road. Crossing when necessary to update on fresh information

Examples of Attack Patrolling

An officer witnesses something and arranges for another officer to go to the point where the suspect is most likely to make off. When in position the first officer attacks and the most likely escape route is covered.

When a robbery takes place the first officer goes to the scene , whilst other officers go to the likely escape routes and in particular the change over points.

The operator of a police vehicle gets out of one end of

an alley and the driver goes round to the other end.

Examples of Trap patrolling

An officer sees a suspect or suspects he wants to stop. The officer follows and uses speed, direction of travel and proximity to encourage suspects to go in direction of colleagues.

Examples of Reinforcement Patrolling

At a known drug dealing location two officers walk through it at unpredictable intervals often shortly after one another, and repeat to deter dealers from operating. It is enhanced when the officers appear from a variety of directions.

At a row of shops where young people cause Anti-social behaviour. An officer gets called to deal with an incident when he leaves and disappears another arrives.

Examples of observing patrolling

Looking down from a tower block at a place where drug deals sometimes occur. Another officer goes to a suitable location to deal with anything the officer sees

The officer sees a person that he is not happy with, perhaps a known thief, but doesn't think he has a power to search based on what he has seen so far, he positions himself in cover and calls on a colleague to come to a nearby location to engage with the person if it becomes necessary

Examples of Link up Patrolling

An officer sees a person who is wanted for violence. The officer links up with a colleague before tackling the person.

In a particular street or estate there is a need to link up, because of the likelihood of violence or numbers of suspects likely to be met.

REASONABLE SUSPICION

The Police and Criminal Evidence Act Codes of Practice says:

Reasonable grounds for suspicion is the legal test which a police officer must satisfy before they can stop and detain individuals or vehicles to search them under powers such as section 1 of PACE (to find stolen or prohibited articles) and section 23 of the Misuse of Drugs Act 1971 (to find controlled drugs). This test must be applied to the particular circumstances in each case and is in two parts:

iii. Firstly, the officer must have formed a genuine suspicion in their own mind that they will find the object for which the search power being exercised allows them to search; and

iv. *Secondly, the suspicion that the object will be found must be reasonable. This means that there must be an objective basis for that suspicion based on facts, information and/or intelligence which are relevant to the likelihood that the object in question will be found, so that a reasonable person would be entitled to reach the same conclusion based on the same facts and information and/or intelligence.*

The problem of course with this guidance is they use the word reasonable in the explanation as to what is meant

by reasonable. I mean what is a reasonable person?
The courts not surprisingly have struggled to define
reasonable, but a reasonable person does not mean the
average, or ordinary person, nor does it mean the ideal
person.

If the courts are confused it's hardly surprising that
officers occasionally get it wrong. I recommend the
following approach. State not only what you saw, but
how and why you interpreted it.

To help you to make solid judgements it helps if you
know what criminals look like. The funny thing is when
you ask the question what does a particular type of
criminal look like you'll get one of two answers, either a
stereotypical description of their appearance, or that
they could be anyone.

Many police officers appear to just know who the
criminals are and can tell them apart from the good
guys. So exactly how do they do this?

What do Criminals look like?
What do criminals look like? is not as stupid question as
it sounds. You'll know from experience that when you
see someone becoming more and more agitated with
somebody else that there is a likelihood it will turn to
violence. If somebody draws their fist back or picks up a
weapon it's becoming even more likely that it will get
violent. There is, in fact, a whole range of signals that a
person will give before striking another. You would
probably be very aware when a situation is about to

become violent because you've learnt to recognise the signs over a long period of time.

It's not just violent criminals that give off signs, all criminals do. You just need to know what to look for. Of course your ability to recognise criminals will be greatly enhanced by intelligence. You should get to know the criminals who live and work in your area. You should know how they behave when they are not committing crime so that you can recognise that they are behaving differently when they are engaged in criminal activity.

Criminals are creatures of habit

Many criminals are creatures of habit. They are performing a job of work, and in that respect are no different from anybody else or does a job or performs any other function.

Take for example the office worker, much of their working life is routine. They will have their favourite modes of travelling to and from work, often doing exactly the same thing on the way buying a paper, sitting in the same seat on a train or bus, or using the same parking space.   Then although the content of their work may differ from day to day, the methods they use, and the equipment they use will usually be the same. They may always check their intray at a certain time such as when they first arrive.   When they sit at a desk they leave clues that they were there, such as the position of the chair, a chewed pen or a bent paper clip.

Criminals are creatures of habit. You will learn a lot about office workers by talking to office workers, and you will learn a lot about criminals by talking to criminals.

BURGLARS

Every burglar will have their preferred method of operating. If they have been successful getting in by approaching from playing fields, climbing over fences, then climbing up the drainpipe into an open bathroom window then that will be their preferred method. Of course if when they climb over the back fence the kitchen door or ground floor window is open they will enter by that means instead.   What they do whilst in the premises, how they prepare for an unexpected return of the occupier, how they conduct the search, what property they take and how they get from house to handler will all be distinctive to the individual burglar.

You may have heard the expression that burglary is an opportunist crime.   There is a degree of truth to this, but a significantly large proportion of burglary is committed by criminals who know they are going to commit a burglary from the moment they get up. Put frankly it's their job.   They know the location they are going to go to, and the type of premise they want to break into. They know how they are going to get in, the property they want to take, and they know what they are going to do with it.

There will always be exceptions to the rule.

Burglars looking for the right property

They will have their preferred method of getting to the area where they intend to work. This may be a car, a van, public transport, a taxi, or on foot. They will park a car or van that allows them to leave the area with minimum fuss. They would not park for instance facing into a cul de sac. Often they will park some distance from where they eventually burgle, especially if they own the car so it is traceable back to them.   They have however also been known to park on the drive of the house they are going to burgle. A stolen car would certainly be less conspicuous on a persons drive than in a quiet residential road. Get to know the burglars who live or work in your beat. Note what they drive and where they usually park when at home.

The burglar arrives in the area where they intend to commit their crime. In the same way that you switch into a different mode when you arrive at work so does the burglar. They start looking for premises that offer them the chance to use their preferred method of entry, and most likely to have the type of property they want to steal. Because they are taking in a lot of information as they walk, their pace is likely to be slower than usual. They may well stash items that will identify them, after all they don't want to accidentally leave solid leads behind. They will stash them in places where they are unlikely to be stumbled on accidently by somebody else, but from where they can retrive them later; for instance behind a green junction box or under a tree stump in woodland.

Burglars clothing

Many burglars dress according to the type of premises they intend to steal from. A burglar who walks into an office block might wear a suit, or at the least clothing that helps them blend in with other people who are lawfully on the premises. One who is stealing from building sites might have a hard hat, and carry a clip board. Some burglars will wear a particularly distinctive piece of clothing in the belief that if it all comes on top and they are seen by a witness then the only thing that they will remember will be the piece of clothing. The burglar of course will discard this and become indistinguishable again.

Some burglars will choose to wear caps, scarves, hoods, or glasses again in the belief that it will shield their face from any witness.   Others will wear two sets of clothing to allow for a change of appearance if it starts to go wrong.

If burglars are carrying tools they may wear clothing that looks out of place in order to conceal what they have.

Tools of the Trade

Many burglars do not carry any tools at all, they figure that either they can gain entry without using force, or that they can get all that they need in the vicinity of the burglary, for instance a brick to smash a window, a garden spade to force a patio door.

Some, however, will carry tools of some form or another. Yale locks can be slipped by the use of "loids' which is basically a flexible, but strong piece of plastic or celloid. Crowbars and screwdrivers can of course also be used to force windows and doors. Improvised fishing rods can be used to hook car keys through letter boxes. Some will have gloves with them, and I've deliberately included these as tools as opposed to clothing. Gloves are tools to prevent the wearer leaving their fingerprints. Much rarer, but still an issue are those that carry weapons in case they are disturbed.

Burglars usually find the bags to carry items from the premises inside the premises they are burgling. Unless they are disturbed they will often leave through the front door.

The burglar is obviously on offer when they are in possession of stolen property. Some may even walk faster. Often they will stash the stolen property quite close to the burgled premises whilst arranging for transport, they may even have rung for a taxi from the burgled property. so it is important to check the last number called from the house.

Consider the different reaction a burglar might have to spotting the uniform of a police officer;

- When on route to the area where they intend to commit their burglary;

- When actively looking for the right premises to burgle within an area;

When leaving the premises with stolen property.

Use your intelligence systems, your local knowledge, your knowledge of crime patterns and criminals to understand how different burglars will react to your presence in the various circumstances.

The drug addict burglar

Many people associate burglary with drug addiction, individuals stealing to feed their habits. Drug addict burglars are certainly easier to catch because their addiction means they take more risks. They leave behind more clues

When a drug addict wakes up the one thing on their mind is getting the next fix. If they haven't got any drugs left or money to buy some they will resort to crime. The drug addict burglar will immediately go to work to get what they need, namely they need to steal property to sell to a handler to get money in order to buy drugs from a dealer.

The drug addict burglar will want to work in one of these areas;

Near their home,

Near the homes of their associates,

Near the home of their partner,

Near their handler,

- Near their dealer,

- An area they have had previous success in

If any of these become 'too hot' because of perceived police activity then they might venture further afield. If such an area produces good returns for little risk then the drug addict burglar will add that to their areas of choice. In choosing such an area they will still be looking for those with the type of premises, and access to those premises where they have had previous success. The drug addict burglar is like a fish in the sea, they will not venture far whilst their needs are being met.   However the more desperate the need the more risks they will take and the more mistakes they will make.

Juvenile burglar

Juvenille burglars often start off by stealing from family, friends, or a local shop, sharing their spoils with a close friend or two, who then become actively involved in their future crimes.

These friends will loiter in the same place for months on end, usually because they live nearby. They will notice people leaving their houses and subconsciously take in the routines of these people. They eventually build up the desire and confidence to commit the crime, having worked out that the risk of being caught is low.

With a successful first burglary under their belt they have increased confidence and an immature belief that they are experts at what they do, so are likely to continue committing crime with their crimes becoming more daring and frequent.

Drunk burglars

Drunk burglars are more impulsive, many would not commit the crime if they were sober, but the drink provides them with the ability to overrule common sense. There actions are often obvious. They often look but do not see, their senses diluted with the effects of alcohol. There is a major problem with being able to spot drunk burglars, because drunks in general do many things that are unusual and out of place. This means that something that otherwise might be suspicious is not registered as such with you because the person is drunk. You need to watch drunks for longer, before you interact with them, to see if they are a drunk burglar.

Night time burglars

Night time burglars are slightly more distinguishable because they are frequently the only person around. They are however hard to spot, because they usually wear dark clothing and understand how light and dark work. Shadows and noise are their friends.

ROBBERS

Street Robbers

Street robbers evolve from school bullies (that's not to say that all school bullies become street robbers.) They operate on being able to control victims who are weaker than them.   Often they work in gangs to help increase this fear factor. Street Robbers need victims to commit crime. Street robbers are in a risky business, so they look for victims who will be too frightened to look at them, too frightened to report them, too frightened to identify them, and too frightened to give evidence against them. To commit their crime they need to go to places where they will find potential victims. Places like shopping centres, inside and outside of schools, parks and around transport hubs.

Because they need to loiter in areas for considerable time until the right victim comes along street robbers will travel considerable distance to find "soft" locations where they are not immediately recognisable by the local police. They also often have non crime ulterior motives for going to different areas, such as to see a relation, or a girlfriend, or to attend a party. They often use the public transport system to get to where they are going. This has the additional benefit of providing the potential for earlier than expected victims.

Street Robbers often wear more than one layer of clothing, and will swap clothing immediately after a robbery to make identification difficult and to cause confusion as to who did what.

A robbery in progress can be very difficult to spot even when its happen right in front of you. It can often appear to an outsider as if its just people talking, whilst in fact the robber is verbally threatening the victim intimidating them and forcing them to hand over their property for fear of assault. It is often the case that a robber will test to see if a person is a suitable victim that they can control, asking questions like "have you got a cigarette?", or "what football team do you support?" How a person reacts will determine whether they become a victim.

You should have an intimate knowledge of robbers who have operated in your area and on the key transport routes that pass through your area.

There may be some benefit in stopping and searching suspected robbers before they commit a crime. It may produce a weapon or property stolen from an earlier crime. It might act as a deterent to some degree, especially if full descriptions of clothing, jewellery and distinguishing marks are taken.

If you approach a group, be aware of anyone that doesn't look like they fit with the others, or is new to the group. Look at their eyes and their body language. They could be a victim. Take them to one side and make sure they are able to talk in confidence with you. Some victims will know their robber, they may even attend the same school, or live on the same estate. In these cases the intimidation and fear may well be far more than can be broken down by this interaction alone. It might be worth following up with a home visit at a later date.

The best way of catching a street robber after they have committed a robbery is by doing a street search with the victim. Remember the robbers often travel by foot or public transport. Don't be in a rush to offload the victim. The likelihood is that the robbers will still be in the neighbourhood.

Ensure that you follow the guidelines in the PACE Codes of Practice for such identifications. Remember the victim is vulnerable and should not be left alone whilst any suspect robber is detained.

Commercial robbers

Robbers who rob commercial premises such as petrol station, betting shops, and corner shops are often street robbers who have decided to go up a "league". They want to "earn" more money than they possibly could as a street robber, and so they choose commercial premises, but they usually select vulnerable premises. Favourites are those with only one or two staff, or where the staff have only limited English language ability. They are often motivated by the need to buy drugs. These ones tend to have not done much preparation, they are desperate and extremely dangerous. They will usually be armed with weapons. They may make some effort to disguise themselves with a scarf or a hood.

Those commercial robbers who are not motivated by the need to get drugs have usually taken up the "trade" through a different route. These criminals will have carried out extensive research into their intended victim. Some will have people helping them on the inside, providing useful information such as when there are less customers, when there are less staff, or when there is larger than usual amounts of cash on the premises. Because they have done extensive research they become harder to spot. They will often arrive and leave in a vehicle driven by a getaway driver. They will operate as an organised gang with the leader recruiting the right people for the job in hand from their network of criminal friends.

They will usually buy everything with cash, and to people not in the know look like successful business people.

This type of commercial robber will often have changeover points where they ditch the vehicle that they used to get away from the premises to get into a new one. usually there will be a physical barrier between the two vehicles such as a footbridge or an alley making it impossible for a pursuing police car to follow. You need to identify potential change over points on your beat, and be suspicious of unlocked vehicles or ones with a driver where the engine running. Also of course be aware of people running in the wrong clothing, at these locations. Remember it may be a bit of time before any victim is able to raise the alarm.

Another form of commercial robber is those that target jewellers arriving and escaping on motorbikes, smashing the shop window and threatening staff and anyone brave enough to intervene with weapons. These have evolved after I left the police so I will not try to tell you how to catch them, other than suggest you identify premises on your patch that might be vulnerable and research those who have been previously caught for this type of offence, and research known criminals that use motorbikes.

DRUG DEALERS

The nature of the drug and the scale of the dealing will dictate how an officer might identify a drug dealer. Intelligence is key. If someone tells you that a person is dealing drugs or a premises is being used for dealing, It makes identifying and catching the dealer that much easier.

When drug dealers of any level are convicted they will usually make the local press. So a good starting point is to carry out research in the local media.

Small scale dealers

Small scale dealers are often addicts themselves. They sell drugs to support their own habit. They will often deal from their own home. This type of dealer can often be recognised by the amount and type of callers they get to their home in a short space of time. They rely on the fact that they only have a small amount of drugs to supply each day, and their ability to conceal the drugs where they will be difficult to find.

Some addicts "allow" others to deal from their premises. Often these are vulnerable people with either physical or mental disabilities. In many cases it is a mutual two way agreement in that the addict gets a drug to use, and the dealer gets to supply their wares from the premises to which there is no paper trail connecting them to them. There are, however, also cases where the vulnerable person is "befriended" and what they think initially as friendship turns into a nightmare over which they have no control.

County lines are an extention of the control street dealers exert over vulnerable people. Like any other successful business a dealer will seek to expand into neighbouring towns and villages until there is a line stretching far from their original base. They are operating like any other business seeking suitable premises to use, and recruiting people to work for them. They will develop levels of management to control activity and security in the form of enforcers that can be shipped in to deal with issues as they arise.

Recruitment of young people into county lines is an essential activity and many of these gangs will have a system in place to ensure that when a potential worker is identified they are headhunted by the person best suited to persuade them to get involved.

One of the essential activities of recruiters and the management structure is to alienate the young person from his family and to undermine any influence that the police and other responsible adults have in their lives.

Creating and getting involved in diversionary activities is an important activity for you to engage in if you are to disrupt county line recruitment activity. Building a bond between young people and yourself will help identify those at risk, and ensure that they get the right level of support.

As you establish that trust you will learn more about the activity of that particular gang, be in a better position to disrupt their activity, and to help vulnerable young people escape from it.

Middle Market Drug Dealers

Middle Market drug dealers are less obvious. They do not have to meet as many people as street level dealers. Some will have made sufficient money from being street dealers to move up the ladder. Others will invest money that they came into legally from a business, from their employment or an inheritence, or illegally from other crimes.

Middle market drug dealers like all criminals give off signs, many will be concerned that they might find themselves under surveillance, and spend a disproportionate amount of time looking for people following them.   To a uniformed officer this can be a big give away. Middle market drug dealers will make unnatural moves such as sudden changes of direction, or going round a roundabout without exiting, leaving a motorway on a slip road, only to immediately rejoin it in the same direction.

On foot they might look behind them frequently to see if they are being followed. Middle market drug dealers will frequent commercial premises that do not appear to get much business. Some of these businesses will be fronts in which to launder money, others will be owned by the person they get their supply from.

You need to know the businesses in your area, and have good knowledge of the quantity and quality of their customers.

Top Tier Drug Dealers and Importers

Organised gangs are at the top. The members have usually been life long friends and associates. Often they will have the trappings of wealth. You need to find out through intelligence already in the system who the members are that live or frequent your patch. Make sure you know what vehicles they drive and build up an intelligence picture of them as you go about your daily patrols. Whereas such intelligence might prove useful one day to other agencies, you might also get a lucky break. The more you know about somebody the more likely you are to catch them in the act.

VEHICLE CRIME

Theft of cars

The ways that cars have been stolen has changed considerably over the years as manufacturers improved security and then relaxed it again as they started to make keyless cars. There are currently two main ways of stealing cars;

◆ usng the vehicles own keys; These might be stolen during a burglary, left in the ignition or as a result of a car jacking.

◆ Using a piece of electric equipment called a relay box on keyless cars.

Another change is that over half the stolen cars are never recovered, often being sold through a handler either for parts or for onward selling abroad.

Not surprisingly it is more valuable cars that tend to get stolen. You need to keep abreast of what the latest trends in cars are, both locally and nationally. Many motoring organisations and magazines annually publish the national statistics for models of cars being stolen. You can see the local trends from crime reports.

Keyless cars

Thieves using relay boxes will work in pairs one waving a box near a house hoping to pick up the signal from a fob left within the home and the other standing next to the car they intend to steal with another relay box. When the signal is picked up it tricks the car into unlocking the doors. This design fault is likely to be addressed, but in the meantime see if you can view what a relay box looks like by asking to see one that has been seized, or look for images of them on line.

It is important for you to know the latest techniques used by car thieves. Needless to say individuals will have an interest in cars and in particular the latest models. They may travel to their selected target in a car that they actually own although it might not be registered to them, or they might borrow a car from a friend. They will park very close to the intended crime so that they can escape in the car that they arrived in if disturbed before being able to complete the theft. The two cars will travel in convoy to the handlers. They will use their own car to distract police from the stolen car.

Prior to committing the offences the thieves will cruise the streets in their car looking for suitable targets. Although often the targets are selected in advance. Intelligence plays an important part in identifying both the thieves and the handlers. If caught in the act it is very difficult to prove that the thief intended to sell the car on, rather than just abandon it. As a S12(1) Theft Act 1968 carries a lowly maximum sentence of just 6 months and even aggravated taking carries a mere maximum sentence of 2 years. Thieves are committing a low risk crime that has a financial incentive. You will know your local car thieves because they will be caught time and time again and be in the intelligence system.

Theft of motorcycles

Motorcycles have become more of the target for joyriders, and for those who intend to use them in certain types of crime because of their flexibility as a getaway vehicle.   Thieves will often have either bolt cutters or an angle grinder to cut through any chain or lock.   They will also have tools to aid them in the hot wiring of the ignition. They usually operate close to their home address and will often take the stolen motorcycle to an open space such as a park or car park where they will let others have a go.

If you try to approach a stolen motorcycle in use, the thief will often taunt you before riding off at speed. Make use of your body worn camera to get images of the rider and motor cycle. Even better try to avoid approaching until the person gets off the motor cycle. In particular when there are groups of people sharing a motorcycle in an open space, bide your time and wait until a less experienced member of the group is on the motorcycle.   It's possible that you will have a number of people you can detain for using the motorcycle. When you and any colleagues you round up pounce to make the arrests the person who is currently on the motorcycle is likely to ride off on it before abandoning it. A quick search of the area may turn up the stolen motorcycle. If you don't find it immediately you might find it over the next few days. If you don't recover the motorcycle, you at least, have a number of people for a range of traffic offences.

Theft from motor vehicles

Vehicles left unattended with property inside will always attract attention of thieves. The thief prefers to operate in areas where the owners will be away from their cars for an hour or more, for example, car parks or streets that have parking meters.   The thief has the advantage of knowing when the parking ticket time runs out and can reasonably assume that the car owner will not return until nearer that time.

Thieves that steal from cars prefer to steal from areas where there is less footfall, so are less likely to be trying to steal near the ticket machines or the exit to the shops, and more likely to favour a place far from the exit like the top floor of a multi-storey car parks than the ground level.

Some will go out in a vehicle which they park up and then go on a stealing spree. They will either take stolen items back to their vehicle if it is nearby, or conceal them for later collection.

Those that steal whilst on foot will want to have the property in their possession for as shorter time as possible so will often be walking on a convenient route from their home address to their handler.

Car thieves will often work alone and will be on constant lookout for police and other people who might witness what they are doing. Like so many criminals they often look but do not see. The vehicle they are stealing from will conceal them to people on the other side of it, so they often pay little attention to people who are not on the same side as themselves. To smash a window and steal an item on a back seat takes less than 3 seconds for an experienced thief. You need to look for the tell tale movement in otherwise stationary vehicles as you patrol the streets.

PICKPOCKETS

Pickpockets require a degree of skill and technique. Some work alone and others will work in an organised gang. They like to work where there is a crowd that will surge forward with a specific purpose and desire, like at a bus stop. When a bus arrives the queue will move forward to get on the bus, getting closer to each other.

Lone Pickpocket

The lone pickpocket will have developed a unique style. The likelihood is that they will use something to conceal what they are doing. This might be a large bag or a coat over their arm. The pickpocket will identify their victim whilst the crowd is waiting, positioning themselves behind, but not in their intended victim's personal space. They will however be within striking distance. As the victim and crowd move forward the pickpocket will use the bag or coat to conceal what their free hand is doing which is picking the wallet or purse from the victim. Once they are successful they will put distance as fast as possible between themselves and the victim.

Most lone pickpockets will discard anything but cash as soon as they can. Some will retain things that have value to others such as passports and driving licences. These they will hide somewhere to be picked up later. Pickpockets work hard identifying victims, and will have unsuccessful attempts. They don't like to linger too long in one particular place but they will have their favourite locations to work.

Pickpocket team

Pickpockets that work as a team have set roles. One will be the principle, that is the one that puts hands on and takes the property, another will be a blocker that will block the victim's movement and others will be security or enforcers who will intervene should someone challenge the action of the principle. Security and enforcers are often armed with knives. The principle will hand the stolen property to another team member to deal with almost immediately. This way the principle is not afraid of being challenged.

Whereas the lone pickpocket has to rely on a sudden surge and condensing of the crowd by something known happening, team pickpockets can create this in any moving crowd, for instance in a busy street. The blocker stopping the victim to ask for a light, directions or anything else that will cause the victim to temporarily stop.

Distraction thieves

Although not true pickpockets, there are thieves who specialise from stealing from people who leave their bags unattended for the briefest of moments, often whilst out shopping. They often work as a team identifying the elderly or a mother with a child who, whilst shopping leave their handbag in a shopping trolley. One will distract the victim whilst the other steals the bag. The thief in these cases will have a bag in which to immediately hide the stolen item. The thief will often discard all that they do not want behind a display before leaving the shop.

Thieves in restaurants

Again these are not pickpockets but target the same type of property. People sitting in cafes and restaurants often leave their handbags on the floor next to them. There are thieves that target this sort of victim. They will enter premises, before taking the property while a person is distracted. If working in a team they might create a distraction away from the intended victim to draw their attention while the principle takes the property.

On patrol look for people entering cafes and restaurants but not buying food. Look for individuals carrying bags that are heavier when they leave than they were when they entered.

HANDLERS

Most thieves steal to make money and they do this by selling it on to either unscrupulous individuals or to handlers of stolen property. There are many handlers that operate as legitimate buinesses. An independent cafe or restaurant owner may be very happy to buy shoplifted items well below their true value so that they can cook and sell on to their customers at the market value. A hairdresser might be happy with products that they could use. It would be very hard to prove that the items were stolen so there is little risk. However it is always useful for the patrolling officer to be aware of these types of handlers, because they will, from time to time, also take in items that you will be able to prove are stolen.

Other handlers may take in property to sell wholesale in a foreign country. Certain items are much more expensive in other countries so there is a good mark up for the handler who can get bulk items.

Other handlers either work from home or a business premises. Most will specialise in a particular type of property for instance cameras or power tools.

The advent of online sales sites and boot fairs provide ready markets for these people to sell these items on.

Of course there are handlers that run legitimate businesses, but at the same time will buy stolen property that they can sell through that business.

Pawnbrokers

Pawnbrokers are legitimate businesses that are regulated by the Finance Conduct Authority. They provide loans against the value of the item being pawned. Make sure you fully understand the law with regards to pawnbrokers. Whereas they almost always operate within the law, they are very vulnerable to thieves pawning stolen items. Establishing a good relationship with them will be an advantage to both the police and the pawnbrokers. Just seeing a police presence regularly in a pawnbroker will make it harder for thieves to abuse the services that they offer. Always fully investigate any pawn receipts you recover during searches of the homes of drug dealer or thieves.

SEX OFFENDERS

Make sure you know who the sex offenders are that live on your patch and the conditions they must comply with. Respond quickly to any breaches. If your force has an individual or team responsible for maintaining and enforcing the register, make sure you regularly speak with them about the offenders living in your area. Provide them with any update intelligence that you are able to garner, such as any vehicle they are using, or just sightings of them out and about.

Of course if they haven't yet been caught a sex offender will not be on the register. Identifying these ones can be extremely difficult as whether they are strangers to, or a life long friend of, the victim, they will be not be displaying anything out of the ordinary, until immediately before the attack. You will need to be aware of anyone who looks uncomfortable in somebody else's company, and check that they are alright by observing and where appropriate speaking to them.

Flashers

Flashers are loners and will choose quiet locations where they will be able to perform the act without interuption. They will wait in areas where there is a good likelihood of suitable victims passing through.

Quiet roads and alleyways near transport hubs. on footpaths or routes in open spaces such as parks, or woodlands are typical haunts for flashers. At this sort of location they can wait patiently for suitable victims to walk towards them whilst at the same time they will have sufficient vision to be able to see anyone who might disturb their offending.

Again other than loitering you may not notice anything that you can act on until they do the act. That said if you know where and when other flashings have happened you may have relevant descriptions and information about the vehicle they use. Flashers will often have tissues available to use after they perform their act.

GRAFFITI

Many people associate graffiti with large gangs loitering in the same place for a long time. Nothing could be further from the truth. Some operate alone and others work in small teams. They are part of a culture that spans the world and has its own music and rules. Many people who commit graffiti have their own social media sites where they are happy to show off their work and even display images or videos of themselves at work.

Often such sites will have links to other sites including close friends and girlfriends who will refer to them by their proper name and give away important information about them.

The tools of their trade are permanent markers and spray paint

Taggers

School aged graffiti artists will often tag their school exercise books, and local areas such as their local park or alley, nearby lamp posts or street furniture. Many young people will know the true identity of a particular tagger, which is another good reason to run diversionary activities and gain the trust of the young people in your area.

Graffiti artists

Bigger works of graffiti, known as blow ups, are likely to be made at night. The graffiti artist concerned with these will often see themselves on a well planned mission. They will have spent some time designing the work and will have a blueprint of it with them.   They will often wear dark clothing and have been known to wear balaclavas.

Graffiti artists, in particular the ones involved in blow ups are not necessarily teenagers.

RESEARCH

Research is so often neglected by police officers. I've lost count of the "intelligence" led briefings that have informed me that there has been an increase in a particular crime, that there were so many in the past month with the preferred times being "whatever."

This "intelligence" is practically worthless to you. Based on it you could end up patrolling an area at a time and place where the active criminals have no intention of committing a crime.

Too often the data is not properly analysed to work out exactly what is going on. Crimes are lumped together according to their classifications. Burglaries with similar methods, where similar property is being taken need to be looked at in isolation, from other burglaries.

If you are not getting proper analysis then you need to do it yourself. Check all the crimes that occur in your area, look for both similarities and differences. Visit the locations and identify the common factors in them. Make enquiries with neighbours, interrogate your intelligence systems and crime databases. Who has been arrested for similar crimes in the past? Were there events going on that might have attracted criminals to an area on a particular day or for a particular time? Are these regular events? Might the same happen next time one occurs? Check shops that take in second hand goods. Are any known names or addresses appearing in their records?

Perhaps the best bit of research you can do, however, is to ask members of the criminal community and their families.

Criminals in general conversation with you will unwittingly drop others in it. They will tell you who the active robbers and burglars are, who is selling drugs, who is violent. Sometimes you will get this type of information in a formal way and you will need to register the criminal as a CHIS, but often you'll get a snippet of info.

The criminal's mother telling you to leave her boy alone everybody knows so and so is doing that shouldn't be ignored, but researched to see if there is any corroboration.

Use all the research tools available to you. The internet for example provides wonderful opportunities to locate people and information. It doesn't matter why you are conducting the research the more extensive it is, the fuller the picture you will have in which to base your decisions. But before you start jumping to decisions you'll need to analyse that research. That means you make sense of what you know and you identify gaps in your knowledge. Where possible you should look for ways of filling thos gaps before making any decision.

OWN YOUR BEAT

It is essential that you "own" your beat. How you tackle any particular issue should be consistent. You have discretion when it comes to enforcing most laws, you need to use that discretion wisely. Just because somebody is providing you information isn't a good reason to let them get away with a criminal act themselves. You want to be, and be seen to be fair in all your dealings.

Don't pick fights you cannot win. Seek help and advice from colleagues who have tackled similar problems to the ones you are dealing with. Learn what worked for them as well as what didn't go so well.

Seek specialist help when the need arises. Don't try to solve everything yourself. Make sure both the law abiding and the criminals know that you are in charge. Do not try to over achieve. Your personal pride should mean that your overall aim is to stop all crime on your beat. However, the aim you relay to the public should be something that is challenging yet 100% achievable.

You should strive to be the "go to" person for any other officer or agency intending to take enforcement action in your area. You should know the history of your area, when it was built, how the demographics have changed over the years and why. You should also be aware of all the major crimes or incidents that have occurred in the area. You should live, breath and smell your neighbourhood. You should always talk about your beat in a positive way. Talk the town up.

GIVING EVIDENCE

Giving evidence in court is for many a daunting experience. You know that, even if your evidence plays only a small part in the case, it is likely to be challenged, otherwise there would be no point in requiring you to be there in person.
Even if you have been to court many times the prospect of being cross examined can for many cause feelings of anxiousness and self doubt. You can make the experience more positive by following these simple guidelines.

You are at court to tell the truth, so tell it.

As a police officer it is important to understand that there will be different versions of the truth. You may witness an incident, but your brain will fill in the gaps to make sense of what you are witnessing. Others witnessing the same event might have different gaps and fill them in differently. This is perfectly normal. When you try to recall those events at a later date you might not remember every single detail. If you try to guess you may well find yourself in difficulty.

Start thinking about giving evidence the moment you start witnessing an incident. If you can, film it. Alternatively make contemporaneous notes of what you are witnessing, and if you cannot do that make some notes as soon as feasible after the event.

Whenever possible and whenever relevant make the notes back at the scene. This is especially important, if you or other parties including the arrested parties were moving in some way, for example during a chase or a fight.

If you chased someone draw a simple map of the route taken. Include where you were when you lost sight and regained sight of the suspect, show when they did something such as when they discard an object.   Use drawings, and descriptive language to help explain. Note features such as door numbers, street furniture the kerb edge, that will help pinpoint where something happened. At the scene check distances, and timings.

Your notes are exactly that, notes that will help you recall exactly what happened. If you write them at the scene they will be more accurate and come your turn to give evidence more useful to you.

Colours can be deceptive. Be aware that under different lighting conditions colours change in appearance. They also change depending on what colours they are next to.   Make a note of such changes.

Be precise in how you describe actions and objects. Don't just write "I saw the person throw a small object away." Rather go into the detail of how they threw it. What hand what was it in? What movement did the arm make? How high? How low? Was it over arm or under arm? What moment did they release their grip of the item?   What was the flight path and how long was it in flight and where did it land, or where did you lose sight of it?   It's all in the detail.   If you put the detail in, a defence lawyer will have less questions to ask you.

When you come to write your evidential statement you will want to put into words the notes that you made in particular the drawings.

Although it will not be possible in all cases, where it is you should revisit the scene shortly before attending court. This will help you remember precise details about the location, even if they are not included in your very detailed notes.

Make sure that you comply with any disclosure requirements, and that you have all the relevant paperwork and exhibits. Don't let criminals get away with their crimes on technicalities that could have been avoided.

When you are travelling to and from court be aware that jury members may be using the same mode of transport, so always maintain a professional demeanour, and never discuss the case in public.

Use the time waiting to be called to give evidence to refresh your memory from your notes and statement.

When you are called to give evidence, enter the court with purpose but do not rush, take your time to enter the witness box. This is your moment, centre stage, you should not allow yourself to feel flustered or in a hurry.

In Crown Court trials you should direct your answers to the jury. It is really important that you listen to the questions being asked. If you do not understand them or you do not know the answer say so.

Defence lawyers are not your enemy, they are representing their clients version of events. They have a job to do and may not like the defendant any more than you do. They may think that the defendant is lying and hasn't got a chance of being believed. It is important that you do not take cross examining by the defence as a personal attack.

Defence lawyers spend a lot of time looking for gaps in the evidence, that they can then exploit to the defendant's advantage. They will have meticulously planned their questions, and the order of those questions to give them the best chance of undermining your evidence. You will have made their job harder by being so detailed in your notes and statement.

You may be asked to reply to a question with a simple yes or no. Most questions you are asked will need for the context to be established so don't be tempted to start your answer with a yes or no, you will be cut off immediately and you will not able to put the context to your answer or otherwise elaborate on it.

Another ploy of the defence lawyer is to change a word or two or to add a pause, in what the defendant is alleged to have said to make it sound less significant or to entirely change the meaning. The best way to counteract this is to repeat exactly what you heard the defendant say.

The more times a person hears something the more likely they are to believe it, and juries are made up of people.

If the defence show you a map or a picture, do not agree to the accuracy of it unless you are absolutely certain that it is accurate. Photos can be taken at a particular angle to hide a significant object from view, or taken with a particular lens to make an object appear nearer or further than it actually is. Maps might have a significant feature hidden by the key. Let the court know what concerns you, that you are not confident with the accuracy or integrity, and even suggest a scene visit. If you yourself have done that visit as I suggested, you will probably know what is conveniently being concealed, and be in position to state what is missing.

PROJECT MANAGEMENT

Project management is about dividing a big piece of work in to smaller chunks of manageable work. Even a very small project needs to be managed to get the maximum effect and value.

Firstly what do I mean by a project in policing terms? It takes in a wide range of activities, including the planning and execution of a warrant, the investigation of a crime, the setting up of a diversionary activity, a crime prevention event or talk.

Regardless the size of your project you will need to have a clearly defined SMART aim.

Specific

Measurable

Achievable

Relevant

Timely

Projects are constrained by three interdependable variables. Scope, Time and Cost. They are often conflicting. If you change the budget, then it will have an effect on the time and scope, similarly change the timescale and the budget and scope will need to alter accordingly. Of course change the scope and it will have an effect on budget and time.

Lets work through a simple example;

At a location you have a large plant container overgrown with weeds owned by the local authority. It is an eyesore. You are aware that the council do not have the funds or desire to do anything with it. You decide to run a project to make the area look better. You can do this by either removing the container entirely or by planting a few plants in it. You decide that the container is worthy of keeping and that your project should have the aim of growing plants in it.

You'll need to ask yourself how much time can you devote to this project. Who can help you? How much will it cost? How will the plants be looked after once they are planted?

The project could of course be completed in the day you thought of it in a very short space of time by going to a garden centre, buying the plants, plucking the weeds out, then planting what you have bought. You could then water the plants on a regular basis yourself.

The project would have been managed. It's cost you time and money, but the scope was limited. You have merely made the container look better.

By devoting a little more time you could reduce the cost and increase the scope. For example you could involve the local primary school in designing what the finished container should look like, and get them involved in the planting. Now when you go to the garden centre instead of buying the plants tell the owner what you want them for and ask them if they are willing to donate them, in return you will put that information into a press release.

You could also suggest that the garden centre display the pupils' garden designs in the centre to the attract the children's parents. You could also involve a local resident to help out by watering the plant.

To complete this project you will need to break it down into its component parts.

- Get agreement from the owner of the container for the project

- Weed the container

- Arrange dates for the pupils to design the planting scheme and to actually do the planting.

- Visit the school to work with the children on the designs

- Identify a garden centre who will come on board and donate the plants.

- Visit the garden centre to collect plants and deliver designs

- Identify a person willing to regularly water the plants.

- Arrange press release

- Arrange photographer

Now set a timescale for each component part. You will see that some of the components require a different one to be completed before they can be done. For example you cannot do the planting until the plants have been obtained. Some however, are not reliant on others. You could, for example, identify the person who is going to water the plants at any stage of the process.

Now that you know how long each component takes you can work out how long it will take to complete the project and therefore set a completion date.

With bigger projects the project manager will be mainly concerned with ensuring others are delivering their component parts on time and on budget. The manager will need to adjust plans or provide additional support to ensure the overall project hits the SMART aim.

This type of project achieves many of the things that the police need to do. It engages young people at an early stage, installing a sense of ownership and pride in their local area. It gives a positive image of the police. It allows adults to see young people in a positive light. It forges links between different organisations.

This breaking down of projects into component parts is key, and although I've given an unkempt plant container as the example it can and indeed be applied to all types of policing.

You get information that a person is dealing drugs from an address. You therefore want to secure the conviction of the drug dealer.

Component parts might include looking for corroboration of the information, by talking to neighbours, and professionals who might be able to provide useful additional information , looking for evidence of drug misuse in the vicinity, researching the known occupants, carrying out observations. They would also include getting the relevant authority for the search, obtaining the warrant, the briefing, obtaining any tools or specialist equipment, or officers you might need. once in the premises and indeed afterwards the allocation of resources to the different tasks.

No matter how big the project it becomes manageable by simply breaking it down into small tasks.

PUBLIC SPEAKING

There is an art to public speaking, and the good news is it can be taught. It doesn't matter whether you are going to speak to a group of visiting senior officers, politicians, local residents, a local Brownie group or pre-school kids, the principles are exactly the same.

There are not many people who are naturally confident public speakers. The thought of standing up in front of an audience to deliver a speech sends shivers down the spine of a surprisingly large number of people, even people who are outwardly highly successful. For some it's the fear of saying the wrong thing, for others it's not wanting to be the centre of attention. Many have convinced themselves over many years that they don't like doing it or are no good at it, so avoid it entrenching their beliefs even deeper. It is the case, however, that everyone is capable of delivering a confident public speech.

The first task you must do when invited to speak in public is to identify whether you are the right person to deliver on the subject. There may well be a good reason why you are not suitable to give a talk on a specific subject, or that there is clearly somebody more appropriate who should be approached to deliver in the first instance. Seems strange that my first bit of advice on public speaking is to pass it on to somebody else, but that's because you will be far more comfortable speaking on issues or subjects on which you have intimate knowledge. Of course an audience is more likely to be receptive to the intended messages if they are delivered by someone in whom they have confidence, and who has an in depth knowledge of the subject matter.

Before taking on any form of public speaking you will need to know who your audience is. Who is going to be at the event? What do they already know? What do the want to know? What do they need to know? What are their interests? Do they want local crime statistics, crime prevention advice, information about your role or a specific part of the law? In other words why have you been invited to speak?

Next you'll need to find out how many people will be attending the event. You'll also need to know the timescale. How long are you expected to speak? Are there other speakers? Do you need to speak with them so as to compliment their speeches as opposed to repeating what somebody else has already said?

You'll also need to know the location. Does it have power? Does it have the equipment necessary for your presentation? How do you get into the venue? Is there a separate entrance for speakers? How do you get there? Where can you park?

Knowing your audience, knowing your subject matter and what is expected of you, and knowing that you will arrive safely and timely at the venue are all very important in delivering a confident public speech.

It is of course important to know what messages you want to deliver. It is widely accepted that if you try to deliver more than three some will be lost during delivery, so focus on no more than your three key messages.

A reliable structure is an important element of any speech. There are a number of structures that can be used to deliver a talk. One such structure if you are delivering information is:-

◆ Tell the audience what you are going to talk about

◆ Deliver the Messages

◆ Confirm they have received the messages

another structure which is useful if you are trying to persuade the audience to take some form of action is to:-

◆ identify the problem

◆ explore the problem in more depth

◆ state the solution

◆ invite the audience to take the action suggested by the solution.

Of course there are many other structures and sometimes a speech is not the best way to impart information. Certainly it could often be backed up by the use of visuals such as PowerPoint, or film clips.

PowerPoint

PowerPoint or Keynote are powerful tools to help deliver messages however they are often not used particularly effectively. We have all sat through the presentations where the speaker reads word for word what is written on the screen, often with their back to the audience for most of the time. These presentations tend to have slides overloaded with words.

A successful PowerPoint presentation is achieved by making it the visual and audio tool it is meant to be. Keep it simple sourcing suitable images or films to illustrate points rather than words. Create graphs or charts rather than a slide of figures.

You should know what is on the screen at any given time without the need to look. Look at the audience not the screen. If you must have words on the screen then learn them off by heart instead of reading them   Remember that you are giving a talk and the PowerPoint is there merely to enhance and emphasise points.

Practice delivering your talk, record it and listen to it. Are you delivering it in a way that the audience will receive the key messages you want to deliver. Remember to allow time for the audience to think, and for information to sink in. In other words do not rush.

Load your PowerPoint from a memory stick to the computer you intend to use, or send it to the organiser in advance. Check everything works well before you give your presentation.

Have alternative plans in case some of the technology doesn't work.

As your PowerPoint is mainly visual, you may want to consider writing specific handouts to be taken away by the audience.

Other visual ways to support your presentation

PowerPoint is useful because it is easy to take to different venues, but do consider taking props. If you are doing a talk on drugs for example would it help to show the audience what illegal drugs look like at the point of sale? Talking on the increase of pickpocketing would having a magician pickpocket "stealing" from a member of the audience help? Or perhaps actors showing the different techniques employed?   Showing the audience the type of locks you are referring to in a crime prevention talk would be an improvement on just a picture of them.

The more you plan and practice your talk the more confident you will be when it comes to delivery and the more confident you are the more expert you appear and in turn the more likely the audience are to listen and take in the messages you are delivering.

STATISTICS

When delivering statistics you need to put them in the best light for the purpose you want to use them.

Take for example that there is 31 violent crimes in the month of May.

You could present it in a number of ways for example

◆ 31 violent crimes in May

◆ A violent crime a day last month

◆ x % of all crime last month were violent crimes.

◆ Only one violent crime a day

How you phrase the statistic will help an audience in making sense of it.

Another method would be to ask the audience to state how many violent crimes were reported to police in the last month, they will usually guess well over the top, giving you the opportunity to bring them down to reality.

We'll look further at how to deliver statistics but first a bit about percentages.

Percentages

It is often the case that you will want to refer to percentages when dealing with increases and decreases in crime, or crime related information. This is the formula for working ou the percentage change

$$\text{Percentage change} = \frac{\text{original value} - \text{new value}}{\text{original value}} \times 100$$

By way of an example if there were 15 burglaries this month and 25 burglaries the month before then by what percentage has burglary been reduced?

$$\text{Percentage change} = \frac{25 - 15}{25} \times 100 = 40\%$$

You will normally use a calculator or an online percentage convertor because the statistics you will be using will be less manageable.   You may well end up with percentages with numerous decimal points.   The golden rule is to claim less than what you actually achieved so as not to lay yourself open to criticism. If for example you end up with a reduction of burglaries of 49.842% it is far better to say 49% rather than rounding it up to 50%. The same applies to increases you would be better to round up a 49.2% increase to 50%. It is about integrity by claiming less than you actually achieved people will be less able to criticise. Lets consider this set of statistics for burglary.

	Burglary this year	Burglary last year
January	10	7
Febuary	12	15
March	13	13
April	5	10
May	6	14
June	15	8
July	7	12
August	4	10
September	4	0
October	5	7
November	6	8
December	12	6
Total	99	110

It can be seen that burglaries decreased when the totals for the years are compared, however how would you have presented the statistics to the public in January, June, or September? How will you present them in subsequent years? To maintain integrity you need a degree of consistency, and you'll need to highlight key points.

Quarterly figures would iron out some of the issues, but there is still an increase in the fourth quarter.

	Burglary this year	Burglary last year
First Quarter	35	35
Second Quarter	26	32
Third Quarter	15	22
Forth Quarter	23	21

Six monthly and yearly figures show reductions. So which would you use and how would you present them?

There is of course no right answer. We have to take the rough with the smooth. If we provide statistics in a consistant format then at least we are being honest. Importantly being honest allows you to deliver messages that will be believed.

Lets consider what you might say at a monthly meeting delivering those statistics.

January: We are concerned about the increase and are taking these actions to improve the situation

February: Remember last month we were concerned about an increase in burglary we took the action we said we would and they appear to have had the desired effect.

March: Burglaries are running at the same levels as last year we will be taking the following actions to bring them down.

April: Burglaries are down in April by 50% the actions we are taking appear to be working.

May: Burglaries are down by over 50% we are really on track for substantial reductions year on year.

June: We've had a bad month, but half way through the year and overall we are down 14% on last years figures. We will be taking the following actions.

July: Burglaries are down by almost 50% this month, the actions we are taking appear to be working.

August: Only 4 burglaries this month. Down by over 50% when compared with last year.

September: We only had four burglaries this month the same as in August. Three quarters of the way through the year and we are down 14%

October: 28% reduction this month compared with last year

November 25% reduction this month compare with last year.

December: Burglaries are down 10% on last year. In real terms this means 11 less victims, less than one burglary every 3 days. The actions we intend to take to do better next year are.....

Each time there was a blip, we have been honest and set out what we intended to do to address it. We have lessened the effect of that blip by emphasising the overall picture. When our actions have worked we reiterated that they 'appeared' to be working.

Of course if instead of presenting the statistics to a community group we were arguing for additional resources to tackle the problem we would use the same statistics to argue how bad things are.

If you use the statistics from January and December you could, for instance, put forward a strong case for additional resources for the following January.

For instance; Last January saw a substantial increase in burglaries. This December there was a 50% increase. We need resources to address a seasonal trend to prevent the burglar or burglars from committing crimes in our area.

Whether arguing for more resources or telling people that crime is decreasing the other statistics available to you help to put everything into context. How many people live in your area when compared to how many burglars operating in it for example. Fear of crime surveys and letters of complaint can all be used to support the need for additional resources.

GRAPHS

A table of statistics are all well and good , but it is often useful or indeed necessary to illustrate points using graphs. These can easily be done by using a wizard within excel or similar computer programme.

It is important to use the corect type of graph.

Line graphs

These can be used to show trends, but are most useful when used to chart two dependable variables. e.g miles per an hour. By plotting this type of graph you could with a degree of accuracy predict missing points or predict what would happen in the future or what happened in the past.

Bar Charts

These are used when there are variables which are not dependent on each other with crime.

Pie graphs

These are used to show what fraction or percentage of a whole of something is. With street robbery for instance you might want to show what age groups are victims. A pie graph will give a visual representation of this information

If you use the wrong graph your message will not be clear.

With all graphs you can create the illusion of things being more as you want them to be.

A line graph can have a sharp or shallow gradient depending on how much you stretch the axis.

A bar chart can also be stretched, both lengthways or in height to give a different picture.

With both linegraphs and bar charts there is no need to start at 0, and in many cases the differences will be more apparent if you don't. The choice of colours you use on your graphs will be important to deliver messages or reduce the impact of negative information.

You will usually use a computer to create a graph, but there are other effective ways to create graphs by having physical objects represent the statistics.

FUNDING

Diversionary activities and crime prevention initiatives are important to you if you want to reduce crime.

Funding may be identified either internally within the police or externally through the Home Office, your Police and Crime Commissioner, local authority, or through other organisations or agencies including charities or trust funds set up to provide grants for specific purposes.

Often the role of the police will be to support a bid for funding by another organisation, perhaps by providing relevant information to support their case of a need for what they want to deliver.

However, there will be times when you feel that there is something that you need for your area, if only you had the funds to purchase the goods or service.

Don't forget you are likely to need to get permission from your bosses for what you have in mind.

Often there are specific forms to fill in that are self explanatory. At other times you just need to structure a request. Such a structure should clearly outline the problem, show the research, identify the proposed solution, including how it is to be delivered, by whom and in what timescale, and the financial implications. Importantly the funder will need to know what success will look like. How will they know that their money was spent wisely?

If you are applying for the funding you will want to collate all the relevant information, the crime statistics, the demographics and reports of where similar initiatives have been successful.

It is useful to be able to show success in your area by comparing your outcomes with those of a comparison site, namely an area that won't be effected by what you're doing, but that has similar demographics and problems.

Making use of those around you

It is important to know and make use of those around you. Within your neighbourhood there will be individuals and organisations that you will be able to work with in your task of reducing crime. Schools can often assist in engaging with young people. Equally they can help to fill a police training need. You need to be open minded. Local businesses can provide support in a wide range of ways It might be with providing a young person with work experience, providing low priced printing for a community organisation or for a good cause, funding for crime prevention, or products you need for a project. Funding comes in kind as well as in cash. Make use of both formal and informal volunteers. Informal volunteers might be those that come together for a one off event like a litter pick.

Your role is to identify what there is in your neighbourhood and then to make use of them if ever an opportunity arrives. You should develop partnerships and working relationships with them. You should be putting different organisations in touch with others that could help.

MEETINGS

There are three reason to attend a meeting;

✦ To inform or be informed

✦ To discuss

✦ To decide

If you are invited to a meeting the first thing you need to do is find out its purpose. Are you going to be informed about something, discuss something or decide on something? Ask for a copy of the agenda, and a list of other attendees in advance to help you prepare for the meeting.

You will need to establish whether you are the right person to be attending. Is there a more appropriate person within your organisation that would be better suited to the task.

You should only attend a meeting if you have a part to play in it.

If you haven't attended a meeting before it can be quite daunting. As with everything in life proper preparation is key. You've got an agenda, you know who is attending, now research the participants and the issues on the agenda. The research should of course be thorough. It is far better to know more than is required. Your research into the participants will show you where they have expertise and where they lack knowledge. If they represent an organisation then you might be able to find out things about the policies and strategies that they have to adhere to.

When researching the agenda, mark against each item what function it performs at the meeting. Are they to inform decide or to discuss?

If you are allocated actions as a result of a meeting make sure you are clear exactly what they are, and any timescale they have to be completed within.

Don't wait to recieve the minutes from the meeting before you set about your actions. and don't wait for the next meeting to report back rather let people know you have completed your action and the result of it.

STREET BRIEFINGS

Steet Briefing are quite simply structured meetings in the open air.   They are particularly good at dealing with persistent problems of Anti-Social Behaviour, or in relation to specific crime problems in an area.   They should not be used in relation to a burglary problem, because you are inviting people to meet you on a street corner and a local burglar will know that certain homes are empty because they can see the occupant at the street briefing,

Street briefings work best if you empower the person making the complaints, by getting them to drum up support from the local residents. That is to say give the person a degree of ownership of the problem. A simple way to do this is by providing them with a leaflet for them to distribute to people who might be affected by the disorder indicating the time, date and location of the briefing. Tell them the more people they can get to attend the better. The actual attendance on the day will give you an indication of how concerned local people are by the issues the complainant has raised with you. You might also consider getting the complainant to conduct a simple survey in the area.

As with all public meetings proper planning is key. Research issues that are likely to be raised including total knowledge of the crime levels, and the nature of the crimes. Check local media for other issues that might be raised regardless of whether they are policing matters.

Carry out a health and safety risk assessment.

A street briefing is in many sense an opportunity to explore whether a formal problem solving process would be beneficial.

Invite key people in particular the ward councillors and other relevant local politicians. Consider inviting other relevant local agencies and organisations.

On the day of the meeting visit the street beforehand to ensure that you are aware of any changes, such as roadworks or damage.

At the meeting introduce yourself and thank the complainant for organising it. Give a brief overview of your role, experience and of the crime issues in the area.

Ask the complainant to explain the specific problem.

Encourage others to express their views on the problem.

Once you have a good idea of the problem explore with the audience what success will look like. You will be trying to establish when they will be satisfied that the issues have been sufficiently addressed. If lots of different issues are being raised get them to agree what should be the priority.

Try to come up with a SMART aim that focuses on what they perceive success will look like.

Agree actions that you and any of the participants will undertake.

Agree a way of reporting back the results.

Conduct an after survey using the same methodology as for the initial survey.

Provide the feedback as agreed.

Maintain contact wth the complainant.

Importantly be prepared to deal with any ASB that occurs whilst you are conducting the meeting. Nothing will impress your assembled audience who are complaining about a noisy motor cycle than you seizing it in front of them and reporting the rider for traffic offences.

Another type of street briefing is one after a major incident, for example meeting commuters as they arrive home after a terrorist attack in town, and providing the latest official update to them in person.

Lesson Plan

Date	Duration

Topic

Aim

Objectives

Content and Teacher Activity	Student Activity	Resources required

A sample lesson plan

LOCALISED SURVEYS

A before and after survey is an ideal way to establish whether you have been successful in addressing Anti-Social Behaviour in a specific area. The way questions are worded is of upmost importance. There are great tools on the internet to assist you in compiling a survey. Try not to ask too many questions and keep them simple.

Here are some sample questions but your problem might warrant different ones.

Q) How safe do you feel inside your home? (Circle the most appropriate)

A) Very Safe, Safe, neither safe or unsafe, Unsafe, very unsafe

Q) How safe do you feel in the vicinity of your home during the day? (Circle the most appropriate)

A) Very Safe, Safe, neither safe or unsafe, Unsafe, very unsafe

Q) How safe do you feel in the vicinity of your home during the night? (Circle the most appropriate)

A) Very Safe, Safe, neither safe or unsafe, Unsafe, very unsafe

Q) Have you been a victim of crime in the last 12 months? (Circle the most appropriate)

A) yes, no

Q) What are the key issues you would like the police to prioritise in the vicinity of your home?

A) (free text)

Q) You have identified an issue when does it take place? (Circle all relevant answers)

A) Monday, Tuesday, Wednesday, Thursday, Friday, Saturday, Sunday.

Q) What time does it take place? (Circle all relevant answers)

A)   before 9am, between 9am and 1pm, between 1pm and 5pm, 5pm and 9pm, 9pm and 1am, between 1am and 9am.

Q) Complaints have been made in relation to the following: motor cycles being driven dangerously in the park. How much of a problem do you see this issue?

A) Very big Issue, big issue, small issue, not a problem

It is useful to have details of the people filling in the surveys, but it is not esential. You may also want to consider whether the survey should be completed by everyone in a household or just one individual in each.

You should always ask the same questions before and after. However, in your after survey you might want to ask additional questions or seek quotes. For example:-

Have you noticed an increase in police presence?

Did you attend the street briefing?

What changes to your vicinity have you noticed in the last 3 months?

If you were doing a survey on commercial premises your additional question might be   Have you seen a change in your turnover in the last 3 months? If so by what percentage?

LESSON PLANS

If you are invited to a school, or youth group to do a talk on a subject. It is useful to complete a lesson plan in advance.

A lesson plan defines the aims and objectives of your attendance. It also provides the structure to ensure that they are achieved by breaking the lesson down into manageable sections. It identifies the resources needed to deliver the lesson and how each section is to be delivered.

Another advantage of having a lesson plan is that if asked to do a similar session you will already have a plan to work from. There are plenty of templates online but create a template that fits your needs

Aims are statement of intent, where you want to be by the end of the lesson. Objectives on the other hand should have definable outcomes.

If you are giving a lesson on knife crime your aim might be to reduce knife crime.

Your objectives might be:

1. To raise awareness of the physical harm knives do.

2. To highlight the consequences of being convicted of knife crime.

You're unlikely to know what impact your lesson had on your desired aim. There are too many other things that might influence any reduction or increase. However you should know that each of your objectives has been achieved.

Lesson plans are also useful for audiences of any age where you want to impart information to others.

Lessons are usually better where they are interactive, where there is a high degree of participation. Where people are exploring the issues for themselves and coming up with ideas or solutions.

Young people in particular like hands on activities or dramatic recreation through role play. They like to see samples to be able to look and hold the things that are being talked about. They like to be creative. Break your lesson down into manageable sections and make each section different in how it is delivered. Use resources such as film clips, pictures or props. Use open questions to encourage participation.

Make sure your delivery is appropriate for the age group you are delivering to, and ensure you are being inclusive selecting different individuals to answer questions.

Perhaps most important is double check that you know the subject matter and you are not delivering information that is wrong or out of date.

YOU WON'T CATCH CRIMINALS SITTING IN THE CANTEEN

There will be times when you need to be inside a police station, writing up evidence, reports or researching intelligence, but the sooner you get back on the streets the more chance you will have of catching criminals. You definitely will not catch criminals sitting in the police canteen.   Good Luck in your career, I hope you enjoy it as much as I enjoyed mine.

ABOUT THE AUTHOR

Michael Wearing joined the Metropolitan Police as a cadet in 1976 aged 17.   He retired as a police constable in 2007. Although he did spend a couple of years in the CID, his career was predominately in uniform. He was one of a 100 people awarded by the Mayor of London for his "Outstanding Contribution to London Life" and he was awarded London's Community Police Constable of the Year 2004. With commendations for detective ability, for bravery, for innovation and professionalism, initiative and enthusism, and for devotion to duty. Where ever he worked he reduced crime through innovative means, arresting wrong doers whilst changing the behaviour of those at risk of offending.

www.ingramcontent.com/pod-product-compliance
Lightning Source LLC
Chambersburg PA
CBHW070741250726
48662CB00004B/1606